Marco Island

Our Home...
Our Paradise

Joel Gewirtz

To Judy –

My Best Friend

My One True Love

Turner Publishing Company
412 Broadway • P.O. Box 3101
Paducah, Kentucky 42002-3101
(270) 443-0121
(800) 788-3350

Copyright © 2001 Joel Gewirtz
Publishing Rights: Turner Publishing Company

All Rights Reserved

This book or any part thereof may not be
reproduced without the written consent of
Mr. Joel Gewirtz and Turner Publishing Company.

Turner Publishing Company Staff:
Shelley R. Davidson, Designer

Library of Congress Control Number: 2001097763
ISBN: 1-56311-744-4

Printed in the United States of America.
Limited Edition.

A TRIBUTE TO SIGGI RIEDEMANN: EVERY SUNSET REMINDS US OF THE ETERNITY OF LIFE AND LOVE. — SANDI

Ma, your extraordinary love, ever blossoming, is held dear in our hearts. — Always, your girls

WISHING WONDERFUL MARCO MEMORIES TO OUR GRANDCHILDREN: THOMAS, RYAN, MATTHEW, SEAN, MEGAN, DOUG AND BRET

DEDICATED TO OUR PARENTS FOR INTRODUCING US TO THIS SPECIAL PLACE WE CALL HOME! — THE POPOFF FAMILY

We celebrate our 32nd year on Marco Island, a magical paradise. — Jack and Rene Pensa

COMING HOME – JOEL AND BARBARA

READY TO SAIL THE WATERS OF MARCO ISLAND.

APPRECIATE EVERY DAY AND NEVER TAKE FOR GRANTED THE BEAUTY AROUND YOU. — DR. WILLIAM AND MARILYN GUTIERREZ AND FAMILY

EUGENIA AND JOHN FONDLY COMMEMORATE THEIR IDYLLIC DAYS ON ENCHANTING MARCO.

To our Dad, who loved Pelicans and lived his dreams. – Love from Denise, Tom and David

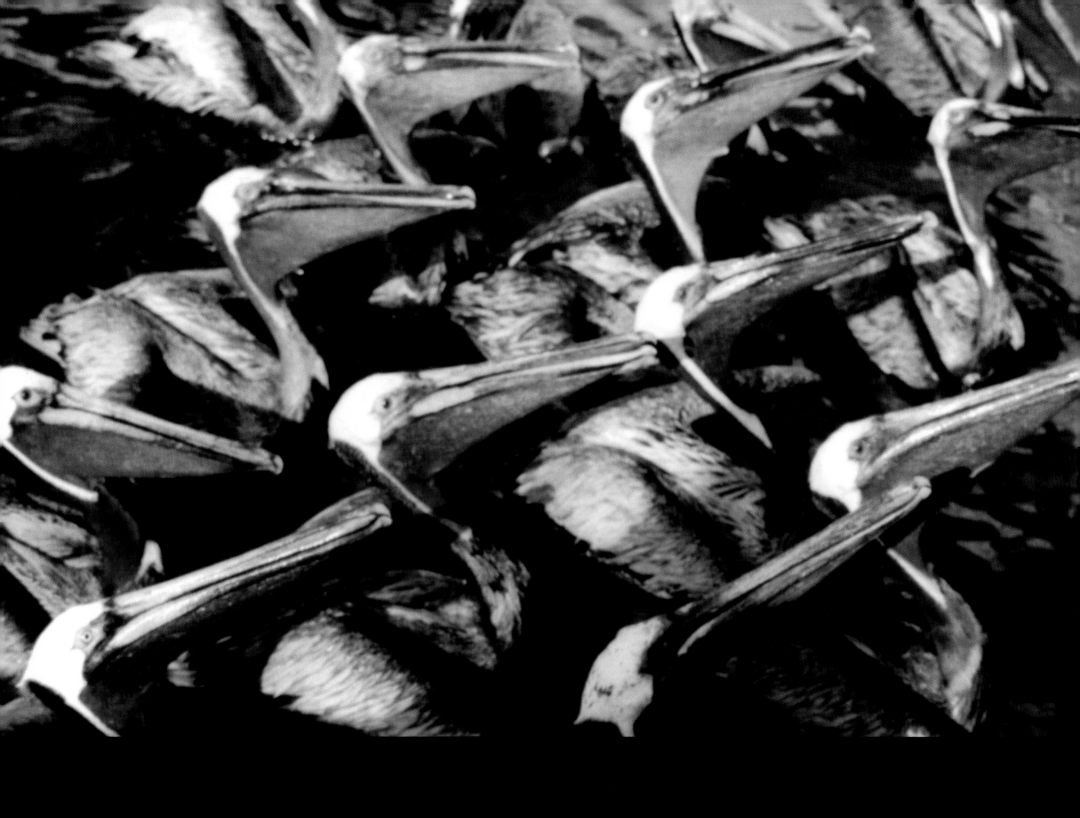

FRED PRELL'S FAVORITE PART OF FISHING WAS FEEDING HIS FRIENDS. — VIRGINIA

MARRIAGE, MOTHERHOOD, MARCO, MANGROVES, MUSIC, MERRIMENT AND MAUI. HAPPY 30TH ANNIVERSARY, GEORGE! — LOVE, RENEE

MARCO ISLAND AND FRIENDS ... OUR GIFT FROM GOD. — MAGGIE, BRYSON AND JOHNNY ANGEL

IN HONOR OF JEAN STORM FAIRLEY AND CHARLOTTE STORM DODGE FROM THEIR LOVING FAMILIES.

MARCO ISLAND... THE ENTRANCE TO THE EVERGLADES... THE BEGINNING OF LIFE. — JERRY MCKENZIE

To Ed Stein, who loved Marco Island as much as we do. In loving memory – Paul and Gayle Stein

In loving memory of Dori McMahon, whose heart was and always will be on Marco Island.

In loving memory of Dorothy M. Rice, who loved life and Marco Island.

Be still and know that I am God ... Psalm 46:10

GOD HAS FILLED OUR SHOES WITH HIS MANY BLESSINGS ON BEAUTIFUL MARCO ISLAND. — PAUL, LINDA, MATTHEW AND BRYAN FLORES

To my friend, Joel, a Marco treasure! — Sandi Marzullo

WORKING IN PARADISE IS LIKE BEING ON A PERMANENT VACATION. — MARCO MOVIES

SERENITY OF GOD'S GIFTS: A PEERING BIRD, MANGROVES, CALM WATERS, REFLECTED COLORS FROM THE SKY. — EVELYN AND TOM OWENS

Don't let the sun set on your dreams. — Jim and Missy Prange and family

Marco Island - a great place to live! — The Finnigans

SAND, SUN AND SUNSCREEN! – ISLAND DERMATOLOGY

CROSSING THE BRIDGE FOR THE FIRST TIME CHANGED OUR FAMILY FOREVER. – MAURICE, JUDITH ANN, TERRY, RYAN AND MAURY

DRIFTING ON THE TRANQUIL CANALS, LOVING TOGETHER, IN THE SERENITY OF MARCO ISLAND. – FRED AND JOY

Sponsors

JOEL GEWIRTZ HAS BEEN TAKING PHOTOGRAPHS FOR NEARLY 30 YEARS. HIS WORK HAS APPEARED IN PUBLICATIONS OF THE MARCO ISLAND CHAMBER OF COMMERCE, LOCAL, NATIONAL AND FOREIGN TOURIST PUBLICATIONS, COMMERCIAL BROCHURES AND DISPLAYS AT THE MARCO ISLAND ART LEAGUE AND LIBRARY. HIS CPA PRACTICE BEGAN IN 1982, BUT HIS LOVE IS PHOTOGRAPHY. HE INVITES YOU TO VISIT HIS GALLERY AT 561 BALD EAGLE DRIVE AND HIS WEBSITE AT WWW.JOELGEWIRTZ.COM.

HE AND HIS WIFE JUDY, ALONG WITH THEIR THREE CHILDREN, HAVE MADE MARCO ISLAND THEIR HOME FOR 19 YEARS. KNOWN AS A VOLUNTEER AT MANY OF THE ISLAND'S ORGANIZATIONS, JOEL HAS BEEN AWARDED THE MARCO ISLAND EAGLE "VOLUNTEER OF THE YEAR."

MARCO ISLAND: OUR HOME, OUR PARADISE IS HIS FIRST BOOK, AND WITH IT HIS DESIRE IS TO CAPTURE THE ESSENCE OF MARCO ISLAND.

WWW.JOELGEWIRTZ.COM
E-MAIL: WALKMARCO@AOL.COM